THE PAGES OF DAY AND NIGHT

ADONIS

THE PAGES
OF
DAY AND NIGHT

TRANSLATED FROM THE ARABIC
BY SAMUEL HAZO

To Rebecca DeBoer —
With my best to you
and yours —

Samuel Hazo
4/17/17

TMP THE MARLBORO PRESS/NORTHWESTERN
NORTHWESTERN UNIVERSITY PRESS
EVANSTON, ILLINOIS

The Marlboro Press/Northwestern
Northwestern University Press
Evanston, Illinois 60208–4210

Printed in the United States of America

ISBN 0-8101-6081-1

Library of Congress Cataloging-in-Publication Data

Adonis, 1930–
    [Poems. English. Selections]
    The pages of day and night / Adonis ; translated from the Arabic by
    Samuel Hazo.
        p. cm.
    ISBN 0-8101-6081-1 (alk. paper)
        I. Hazo, Samuel John. II. Title.

PJ7862.A519 A24 2000
892.7'16—dc21

                                                        00-056638

NOTE

I would like to thank Mirene Ghossein, Kamal Boullata and Antoinette Tuma for providing the literal translations from the Arabic that were the basis for my final transversions, Bradford Morrow for permitting me to reprint as an appendix Esther Allen's translation from the French of Adonis' "Poetry and Apoetical Culture" (CONJUNCTIONS, 19), Austryn Wainhouse for suggesting the final scope of this book and, finally, Adonis himself for his friendship and cooperation. I hope that these versions of his work further enhance his deserved reputation as one of the leading poets (if not the leading poet) in the Arab world today.

Samuel Hazo

CONTENTS

THE PAGES OF DAY AND NIGHT

PREFACE

1.

I write in a language that exiles me. The relationship of an Arab poet to his language is like that of a mother who gives away her son after the first stirrings in her body. If we accept the biblical story of Hagar and Ishmael, as repeated in the Koran, we realize that maternity, paternity and even language itself were all born in exile for the Arab poet. Exile is his mother-country, according to this story. For him it can be said: in the beginning was the exile, not the word. In his struggle against the hell of daily life, the Arab poet's only shelter is the hell of exile.

2.

What I have just said returns us to origins—to myth and to language. Based on these origins, Islam offered a new beginning. It dislodged language from its worldly exile and oriented it to the country of Revelation—to heaven. Through language Revelation reveals the metaphysical while work organizes the physical. This organization has been entrusted to man as the new caliph—the successor of the Prophet. Revelation was instituted at the moment man accepted the charge of putting it into practice. Then it became a law, a system.

Yet in every system there exists another form of exile because every system is both a limitation and a route planned in advance. Every system forces man out of his being and identifies him with his appearance.

Thus, Arab life from its inception has been an exile from language and the religious system. In the past as well as in the present, the Arab poet has known many other forms of exile as well: censorship, interdiction, expulsion, imprisonment and murder.

In this scenario the Other seems to be the salvation of the I. The Other is neither past nor future, nor is it a mirror that is capable of returning the I to childhood. Rather it helps to set the poet in motion toward the unknown, toward everything strange.

3.

From such a perspective, poetry is certainly not a "paradise lost" nor is it a "golden age." On the contrary it is a question that begets another question. Considered as a question, the Other concurs with the I who is actually living the exile of the answer. Therefore, the Other is a constitutive part of the answer—the element of knowledge and Revelation. It is as if the Other is the impulse of the question within the I.

The Other has been omnipresent in the creative experience of Arabic poetry. Because the language the Arab poet uses contains many languages, old and new, Arabic, poetically speaking, is plural but in singular form.

But whether in practice or in its contacts with the aforementioned system, the Arabic language has nothing more to tell us. Rather it has become a language of silence, or rather it tends to reduce expression to silence. Its orbit is muteness, not diction. The Other, the Western persona in this instance, is transformed in his relationship to the Arab poet into a limitation and a chain, at least in reference to the system. He may be content with his own freedom within his own limits. Perhaps he may see nothing in the Arabic past but the answer to a question he knows in advance since he devised the question out of his own imagination, need and interest.

This may explain why the Arab poet embodies a double absence—an absence from himself as well as an absence from the Other. He lives between these two exiles: the internal one and the external one. To paraphrase Sartre, he lives between two hells: the I and the Other.

The I is not I, nor is it the Other.

Absence and exile constitute the only presence.

4.

Being a poet means that I have already written but that I have actually written nothing. Poetry is an act without a beginning or an end. It is really a promise of a beginning, a perpetual beginning.

To be means to mean something. Meanings are only appre-
hended through words. I speak; therefore, I am. My existence
thus and then assumes meaning. It is through this distance and
hope that the Arab poet attempts to speak, i.e., to write, to be-
gin.

But, between the two exiles I have mentioned, is a beginning
really possible?

And, before all else, what is such a beginning?

I ask this question so I can answer it indirectly by saying that
the Arabic language was and is a constant attempt to establish a
beginning which cannot be established because its establishment
seems impossible.

And since poetry by definition is on the side of presence, the
Arab poet cannot live nor can he write within the illusion of a
possible foundation. In his life and language, the Arab poet thus
speaks ever of freedom and democracy as illusions.

I say *illusion* because life itself comes before freedom and
democracy. How can I possibly talk about life when I am
prevented from being myself, when I am not living, neither
within myself nor for myself, when I am not even living for the
Other?

The problem of freedom for the Arab poet (unlike his Other,
his western counterpart) does not reside in the awakening of indi-
viduality or in the partial or total absence of democracy and hu-
man rights. Rather the problem resides in what is deeper, more
remote and complex because, ironically, it is simpler. It resides in
the primitive and primordial. It resides in man's original exile, in
what constitutes and is constituted, in the No of what orders and
prohibits. This is the No that not only creates culture but also cre-
ates man and life itself.

5.

Institutionalized language overflows the I and the Other and
shakes the very foundations of freedom and democracy. It is the
language of death and massacre where both the I and the Other
discover their deaths.

Death sees nothing but death. The I that is already dead cannot accept the Other but will only see him in his own image, which is the image of death. Our poetry at present seems to be moving within this kind of death.

Adonis
Paris, 9/3/92

THE PASSAGE

I sought to share
the life of snow
and fire.
        But neither
snow nor fire
took me in.
        So
I kept my peace,
waiting like flowers,
staying like stones.
In love I lost
myself.
        I broke away
and watched until
I swayed like a wave
between the life
I dreamed and the changing
dream I lived

THE DAYS

My eyes are tired, tired of days,
tired regardless of days.
Still, must I drill
through wall after wall
of days to seek another day
Is there? Is there another day?

THE WANDERER

A wanderer, I make a prayer
of dust.
        Exiled, I sing
my soul until the world
burns to my chants
as to a miracle.
                Thus am I
risen.
        Thus I am redeemed.

THE MARK OF SISYPHUS

Others I know. Against
them I fling the penance
of this rock before I turn
to face the time to come.
The innocent years revolve
like life within a womb.

I see in the west a light
of green frontiers where I
may never find my other
self. I turn from men,
shoulder tomorrow's sun
and bear it forward to heaven.

THE SLEEP OF HANDS

Today I offer my palms
to dead lands and muted
streets before death seams
my eyelids, sews me
in the skin of all the earth
and sleeps forever in my hands.

UNDERGROUND

The presence of cities
passed between the lashes
of our eyes.
                    Behind
our faces' counterfaces,
we shouted like the lost,
"In every city's catacombs
we live like snails
within their shells
                    O cities
of rejection, come!
Discover us!"

TREE OF FIRE

The tree by the river
is weeping leaves.
It strews the shore
with tear after tear.
It reads to the river
its prophecy of fire.
I am that final
leaf that no one
sees.
      My people
have died as fires
die—without a trace.

THE CAPTIVE

Imprisoned by the buds and grass,
I build an island in my mind
by weaving branches from a shore.
Harbors dissolve. Black lines
unweave themselves. I pass

between the barriers and springs
of light that made my dream.
I feel the jailed astonishment
of every butterfly that falters
in a fluttering of dying wings.

HUNGER

The hungry planted a forest
where weeping became trees,
and branches . . . a country
for women in labor.

A harvest of unborn children
grew like buds from the bed
of this the universe.
The forest turned to ashes

with their cries that came
as if from towers of disaster
bearing the small, starved voices
accusing, accusing, accusing.

Listen
          Let me tell
you my dream.
                    I saw
a child driving the wind
and stones as if through water.
Under the water were bounties
locked as kernels are locked
in a rush of becoming.
But why did I sorrow like hymns
from the kingdom of famine
and tears?
                    Listen!
I'm calling you to recognize my
voice.
               I am your
prodigal brother riding
the stallion of death to find
the door marked destiny.

Each day is a child
who dies behind a wall
turning its face to the wall's
corners.
        Houses flee
before its ghost that rises
from the grave demanding
vengeance.
        Not from eternity
but from a bitter land
it comes, fleeing as if from bullets
through the town, the public
squares, the houses of the poor.
From the desert it comes,
and on its face is the hunger
of pigeons and parching flowers.

Through overnetting clouds
plunged two stars.
I stopped and bowed,
acknowledging their greeting.
Still the palm tree
shook and shook
its sculpted leaves like some
old scribe of sorrow,
now moved, now
chosen to record and see
(within the barriers
that no one sees)
how space begins with trees
and how, above
them to the stars
. . . only the wind, the wind, the wind.

THE CALL

My morning love,
meet me in the sad field.
Meet me on the road
where the dried trees
shielded us like children
under their dried shadows.

Do you see the branches?
Do you hear the call
of the branches?
Their young shoots are words
that strengthen my eyes
with a strength
that can split stone.

Meet me. Meet me,
as if we had already dressed
and come and knocked
on the woven door of darkness,
parted a curtain,
flung windows open
and retreated to the sinuosities
of branches—
as if we had poured
from the brims of our eyelids
such dreams, such tears—
as if we had stayed
in a country of branches
and never chose to return.

Leave me alone.
Let birds come.
Let stones be laid on stones.
Leave me alone.
I waken streets
when I walk through processions
of trees.
        Under branches
I remember journeys
when I rose to foreign
suns and let the morning
seal my secrets.
Leave me alone.
A light has always
led me home.
A voice is always calling.

Before the time of day—I am.
Before the wonder of the sun—I burn.
Trees run behind me.
Blossoms walk in my shadow.
But still tomorrow
builds into my face
such island fortresses
of silence that words find
not a door to enter by.
The pitying stars ignite
and days forget themselves
in my bed.
          The springs within my chest
are closing now like blossoms
to the moon.
          Their waters bathe
the mirror of my vision pure
as silence as I waken into sleep.

A TREE

I carry no sword.
I've never sculpted a head.
In summer and winter
I am a bird fleeing
in a torrent of hunger
to an empty nest.

My kingdom is a road
of water.
In every absence I am present.
In pain or shyness,
in rain or dryness,
far or near—
I possess the light of things.

And when I go,
I close the door of the earth
behind me.

1. The Wave

Khalida,
you are a branch in leaf—
a voyage that drowns each day
in the fountains of your eyes—
a wave that helps me see
how starlight,
clouds
and sands beneath a wind
are one.

2. Underwater

We sleep beneath a cloth
woven from the harvests
of the night.
O night of dust . . .
Cymbals and alleluias
chorus
in our blood.
Underwater suns
glitter
the dark to dawn.

3. Lost

. . . once,
encircled by your arms,
I lost my way.
My lips were fortresses
succumbing to a conquest
they desired.
Nearer,
nearer you breathed,
your waist—a sultan,

your hands—the messengers
of armies in reserve,
your eyes—lovers
in hiding.
Joined,
lost together,
we dared a forest of fire,
me—risking the first step
toward it
you—pointing the way.

4. *Fatigue*

Darling, an old fatigue
invades our house.
It looms in every drawer
and balcony.
It waits until you sleep
before it vanishes.
How anxious I become
about its going and coming.
I scout the house,
interrogate the plants,
pray for a glimpse of it
and wonder how, why, where.
The winds,
the branches
come and go.
But you—never.

5. Death

After our seconds together
time turns back to time.
I hear footsteps
repeated
down a road.
The house is nothing
but a house.
The bed forgets the fire
of its past and dies.
Pillows are only pillows
now.

A MIRROR FOR MY BODY IN LOVE

When my body loves,
it melts the day in its tornado.
Perfumes come
to its bed where dreams
vanish like incense
and, like incense, return.

The songs of grieving children
are the songs my body sings.
Lost, bewildered on a dream
of bridges, I ignore
the soaring road that crosses me
from shore to shore.

A DREAM FOR ANY MAN

I live in the face of a woman
who lives in a wave—
a surging wave
that finds a shore
lost like a harbor under shells.

I live in the face of a woman
who loses me
so she can be
the lighthouse waiting
in my mad and navigating blood.

"Who are you?"
                    "Say I'm a clown in exile,
          a son from the tribe of time and the devil."
"Was it you who solved my body?"
                    "Only in passing."
"What did you find?"
                    "My death."
"Is that why you hurried to bathe and dress?
When you lay nude, I read my face in yours.
I was the sun and shadow in your eyes,
the shadow and the sun. I let
you memorize me like a man from hiding."
                    "You knew I watched?"
"But what did you learn about me?
Do you understand me now?"
                    "No."
"Did I please you, leave you less afraid?"
                    "Yes."
"Don't you know me then?"
                    "No. Do you?"

VOICES

1.

O my dreams, my dancers,
come in, come in.
Salute the now and here.

Stir my pen to paper.
Say that life
is more than merely living.
Come.
Leaven the bread of my words.

2.

The sun showed me its journal.
The white ink of my tears
chaptered my history
on those black pages.

The last of all doors
opened,
and I saw my buried days,
the shrouds of my innocence.

3.

Where did the light go?
Did the wind make off with it?
Why did it flee
like a refugee among the trees,
stumbling through mud,
washing itself of day,
rising through seclusions
to hide beneath the skin
of the once more pregnant sun?

4.

Why call me man?
That's not my name.
Why bother with identity?
Just say I live
in the closed drum of space.
If you must say something,
say that.

5.

With echoes for neighbors
we will die together
and live in the shadow of seasons,
in dust,
in the open book of prairies,
in grass we trampled once
and signed with our footprints.

We will stay like relics
of our kind
for our kind—
reminders, shadows,
echoes of echoes.

6.

Mihyar assembles space
and spins it on his tray.
He towers over everything.
Nights are his paths,
and stars are his fires.

One look at his face—
and the sky brightens.

7.

If I called the winds,
would they suspect me?

If I dreamed that they
and not the earth
should bound my world,
would they admit me
to the royalty of eagles?

If I deceived the winds
and stole their keys,
would they destroy me?

Or would they come to me
at dawn—
even as I slept—
and let me dream
on, on.
. . . on

1. A Dream of Death

When I saw death on a road,
I saw my face in his.
My thoughts resembled locomotives
straining out of fog
and into fog.
Suddenly I felt akin
to lightning
or a message
scratched in dust.

2. A Dream of the Sea

Mihyar is a poem
to wound the night of the tomb
with light
as brightly as the sun unveils
the face of the sea,
wave by
wave by
wave.

3. A Dream of Poetry

I hear the voice of time in poems,
in the touch of hands, here, there,
in eyes that ask me
if the eglantine shall shut
the door of its hut
or open another.

. . . a touch of hands, here, there,
and the gap from infancy
to immolation disappears
as if a star emerged
at once
from nowhere
and returned the world
to innocence.

A KING, MIHYAR

Mihyar, the king . . .
alive in a dream of castles, gardens
and days in service to his words.

A voice, buried . . .
Mihyar's, the king's. . . .
He rules the kingdom of the wind
and keeps his secrets.

HIS VOICE

Mihyar, betrayed by friends,
you are an unrung bell,
two syllables on lips,
a song recalled
on the white roads of exile,
a gong sounding
for the fallen of the earth.

MOUNT SUNEEN

From his room in the sky
my mountain
reads
to the night
to the trees,
to all who cannot sleep—
his high sorrows.

A WORLD OF MAGIC

Between the lord of days and me—
no hatred, no vendetta.
Everything's over.
He's barricaded time
behind a palisade of clouds.

My world goes on as magically
as ever. I contradict
the wind. I scar
the waves before I scurry
from my bottle in the sea.

PRESENCE

The door I open on the world
ignites the present
under battling clouds
that track each other
over oceans spined with waves,
over mountains, forests, rocks.

From roots and ashes I create
a country for the night
and watch it grow.
Fields fountain into song.
Flaring out of thunder, lightning
burns the mummies of the centuries.

FINALLY

For once,
for the last time,
I dream of falling in space . . .
I live surrounded by colors,
simply,
like any man.
I marry the blind gods
and the gods of vision
for the last time.

THE TRAVELER

The glass shade of my lamp
reflects me
even after I'm gone.
My gospel is denial,
and my map—
a world I've yet to make.

DEATH

"We must make gods or die.
We must kill gods or die,"
whisper the lost stones
in their lost kingdom.

THUNDERBOLT

My green thunderbolt,
my spouse in the sun,
my madness,
change the face of things.
I've fallen under rocks.
I'm blinded and beseeching
in a land without a sky.

Possessed at times
by hell and gods,
I am an eagle
winged with wind.
I leaven seeds in soil.
I bend the bow
of the nearest cloud.

O my thunderbolt,
change everything,
change all the maps.
Be in a flash
my likeness in the sun,
my twin in madness.

ADAM

Choking quietly
with pain,
Adam whispered to me,
"I am not the father
of the world.
            I had
no glimpse of paradise.
Take me to God."

A MEMORY OF WINGS

Icarus passed here.
He pitched his tent
beneath these leaves,
breathed fire in the green chambers
of the frailest buds
and shuddered and sighed.

Tense as a shuttle,
he drank himself dizzy.
and flew for the sun.

He never burned.
He never returned,
this Icarus.

THE SONG

Strangled mute
with syllables,
voiceless,
with no language
but the moaning
of the earth,

my song discovers death
in the sick joy
of everything that is
for anyone who listens.
Refusal is my melody.
Words are my life,
and life is my disease.

THE MARTYR IN DREAMS

Midnight stares from his eyes.
No longer in his face—
the calmness of palms,
the certitude of stars . . .

The winds, the winds
unshape and shatter on his brow
so many scattered reeds,
such crowns of violence.

SONG OF A MAN IN THE DARK

To ascend? How?
These mountains are not torches.
No stairs await me
in the higher snows.

Thus for you
from here—
these messages of grief . . .

Each time I rise,
the mountains in my blood
say no, and darkness
holds me in its narrow sorrows.

1.

Stripped of seasons, buds and fields,
I leave so little to the sands,
less to the wind
and nothing to the day's hosanna
but the blood of youth.
In tune with heaven,
I hear the chiming of ascending wings
and name the earth my prophet.

Stripped of seasons, buds and fields,
I wake with springs of dust in my blood,
and in my veins,
such love, such yearning . . .

From the sea's floor
my heart sets sail.
My eyes remember oceans.

Here,
banished here,
my life is in my eyes,
and my eyes sustain me.
I live my life out waiting
for the ship of destiny
to rise from its grave.

Is this a dream?
Is there no voyage called return?

2.

Stricken by the cancer of silence,
I scrawl my poems in the sand
with a crow's feather.
My eyes see nothing but lashes—
no love, no sea,
no wisdom but the earth.

With springs of dust in my blood
I sit all day in this cafe
and wait for someone
to remember me.

I want to pray on my knees
to owls with splintered wings,
to embers,
to the winds,
to slaughterhouses and a thousand drunkards,
to stars hidden at the sky's center,
to death by pestilence.

I want to burn the incense
of my days, my songs, my book,
my ink and my inkwell.
I want to pray
to gods that never heard of prayer.

Beirut is invisible.
Nothing blossoms on its mountains,
and nothing blooms on mine.
In the month of figs and apples,
locusts shall devour my fields.

Barren and alone in orchards,
in sun and after sun,
I walk Beirut and never see it.
I claim Beirut and cannot flee it.
As the day passes, I pass,
but I am elsewhere.

3.

These days are mounds of skulls,
rubbish for mongrels.
Without a cross they welcome God
and chant the dead unblessed to burial.

Stricken by the cancer of silence,
I smoke all day in this cafe.
While sails of conquest
streak the sea,
I stamp my cigarettes to butts
and wait for someone
to remember me.

The festival of rain has passed
from our faces.
                        We've turned
the world to stone.
                        Blink
by blink, our lashes chime us
onward to the broken knot
of heaven.
                        And all, all
I have saved from summers of basil
to the dust of tears remains
this elegy of our defeat.

1.
We blunder through prophecy
as if through sand.
                        "Brother
show us a sign that shall
prevail."
                        History crumbles
downhill like a babble of ants
that choke on their own dust,
on the filth of snails, on shell
after shell . . .
                        In the beginning the moon
was a single eye, and heaven—
the forehead of a viper.
                        Nothing
survived but leprosy in search
of faces it could pock
and hollow.
                        Disemboweled bellies
yawned a scum of mosses.

A pigeon's skull wobbled
on a threshold.
                    Fever burrowed
through a knight's helmet.
                              "You!
What is it you want, Greek?"
"Some dates, my lord, some bread.
My road is endless.
                        Hunger
is a horse neighing through its teeth."
"Bring water for the thirsty
Bring bread for all who flee."
We learned defeat beneath
the flags of dust.
                    Graveyards
bloomed from our faces.
                          We wrote
our testaments in famine.
                            Not
a star glimmered above us.
We scouted the sand for ghosts.
We searched the caves of wind
and tears.
            "O God, we seek
some shelter in the earth.
Let rivers hide us
from the final enemy."
                        Thus chanted
our virgins, while the sea,
like a prophetess, waved
to us and sobbed.
                    Who
could swim from shore to shore?

"Tell us our fortune, mother
of the sea, before the spots
of death speckle our flesh."
The ashes of the dead planets
splashed like water in our eyes.

2.
A mountain speaks its name
to me.
        After all, I have
some credentials.
                But who
can set the price for nation
after nation of us?
                And who
shall bear away our gatherings
as gifts?
        Let him accept
as well each sword and dagger.
Let him take every anklet,
brand and welt.
           We peddled
diamonds in the marketplace
for blind and useless elephants.
A man blessed himself
with the sandal of a king.
             Another
was split, alive.
        A third
escaped on broken legs.
A fourth died of a threat.
A prophet carried his own head.
A man without a name painted

his portrait with camels milk.
A son recognized his mother
at a king's table.
                              A husband
slept with his wife beneath
a prince's cloak, dreaming
in the silks of slavery and fear.
A corpse stuffed with hay
paraded through the streets.
                              A dead
eunuch received seventy
lashes plus ten.
                              A woman
with one breast dared a gauntlet
of eyes.
                       A child wore
vestments to his crucifixion.
The lords of the land were Ahmad,
Cafour and Timurlane.
The father of knights, the musk-
man, the ravishing princes
were our own people.
                              They wore
as crowns the consecrations
of our lives.
                       The stars rained
spittle on us in God's
name.
                  In the name of God
we sailed those years on broken
wings and nailed our foreheads
to a timber.
                       We prayed the ruin

of our land.
                    "O God, let victory
come to our masters
and to their sons.
                    Let them
be lords of all the lands
and all the seas.
                    Let wise men
bring us saviors from abroad.
Let them be men of lightning.
Their names and faces shall be
minted on our coins.
                    Our women
shall sleep on a pillow of lilies."

    3.
Here is a people turning
their very faces to the hoofs.
Here is a land humiliated
like a coward's house.
                    Who shall
tender us a bird, just
a bird?
            Just a tree?
Who shall teach us
the alphabet of air?
                    We wait
at the crossroads.
                    We watch the sand
submerge our beacons.
                    The sun
disintegrates within the wrinkles
of our hands.

O my country . . .
Your skin is a lizard's.
                        Your perfume
is the stench of rubber scorched.
Your sunrise is a weeping bat.
You bring such holocausts
to birth.
                  You give your breasts
to vermine.
                  "Maid, the master
is calling.
                  Bring him coffee
from Mocha.
                        Sheet his bed."
And I, rejection's master,
turn from my window,
shivering, to write my soul.
Tarantula's tears are webbing
my eyes.
                  Death flutes
in my throat.
                        I crown my heart
with a feather.
                        I marry the wind,
and nothing but torn maps
and thunderstorms shall mark
my going.
                  Neither day nor night
shall recognize me.
On the dirt of oblivion my steps
shall grow.
                  I am content
to be a floating corpse.

My life has been one tour
of terror.
        Tonight the dove
of farewell burns in my heart.

   4.

A word without a moon
sounds over us.
             Nightclouds
carry the snow of Christmas.
"Beware and keep away!
Magi and guests, avoid
us while you still have time.
We rule like princes over nothing.
Our history dissolves like foam.
I warn you. Go away."
Mud engulfs us like a net.
We drown in it.
           Slime
covers our eyelids.
             It scarves
our necks like silk.
             Somehow
it came without a cloud.
What happened to the thunder?
Who stilled the prophecies
of havoc?
        "Come then.
               Invade

us
    Invade our sacred
lives.
        Our women wait

for you behind the bushes
of their dreams, in chambers,
on the grass.
                    Their loins and nipples
Stiffen with the aches
of lust.
              You are
their only lover."
                        My country,
are you no more than air,
no dearer than a hill of salt?
Have you been stained too long
with the ashes of scribes?
                        My country,
you are an old soldier.
Like me, you give your very guts
to move ahead.
                    Like me,
you groan with every step.
I mourn with you.
                        I know
how a back breaks.
                        I share
your fate beneath this tree
of my despair, but the roots
of the plague are clear to me.
Blink by blink, I wait
a darker eagle.
                    Behind
my shoulder stands the shepherd
of no hope.
                His flutes break
in my chest.

The road before me
bleeds with nothing but anemone
and weeds.
I hear a rasp
of thorns.
Despair, I call you
by your right name.
We were never
strangers, but I
refuse to walk with you.

5.

Rejection's banners guard
me as I weave these words,
but in my face another
marriage has begun.
I call
the earth my wife.
I free
my captive flesh and bow I
to lightning as a friend.
I bathe
my wounds in thunder.
I murder
that charlatan, the moon.
I ride
a salamander's back abroad
and breathe embers.
Each scorpion
becomes a country in itself.
A frog wears history's mask.
A beggar keeps the books
of glory.

Yet, I feel
such rage here on the earth's
backbone, learning the sweetness
of all hidden and forbidden
things.
                    I scrawl the history
of time's beginnings.
                                        While
the sun's nail nicks
my check, I mate the languages
of rain and ink.
                        I let
Cain feel proud of his grandson.

    6.
Stones turn green.
                            I step
toward the risen light.
Each star dies in the sea.
An iguana flirts with heaven.
A peak erupts with smoke
and snow.
                    I herald a day
that never came.
                                "Poet!
Rise from your cave.
                            Forget
the salamanders, rats and worms.
Come out.
                    Witness.
                                    Testify.
The land that had a name
is nameless.

Corpses lie
everywhere.
                    After sudden
death, come out and speak
your promise to the sea and sky."

    7.
Behind the veils of prophecy
we whispered, "Brother, give
us a sign that shall prevail."

    8.
Drawn forth to silence
by the drum of words, I am
a knight riding the horse
of all the earth.
                    My song
is everything I see and all
I breathe.
                    Under thundering
suns, I pace the foaming
shore.
                    I sing my way
to death, and, having sung,
I leave this elegy to burn
for poets, birds and everything
alive from here and now
until the end of heaven.

1.

Chanting of banishment,
exhaling flame,
the carriages of exile
breach the walls.

Or are these carriages
the battering sighs of my verses?

Cyclones have crushed us.
Sprawled in the ashes of our days,
we glimpse our souls
passing
on the sword's glint
or at the peaks of helmets.

An autumn of salt spray
settles on our wounds.
No tree can bud.
No spring . . .

Now in the final act,
disaster tows our history
toward us on its face.
What is our past
but memories pierced like deserts
prickled with cactus?
What streams can wash it?
It reeks with the musk
of spinsters and widows
back from pilgrimage.
The sweat of dervishes
begrimes it as they twirl
their blurring trousers into miracles.

Now blooms the spring of the locust.
Over the dead nightingales
the night itself weighs and weighs.
The day inches to birth
while the shut and bolted door
of the sea
rejects us.

We scream.
We dream of weeping,
but tears refuse our eyes.
We twist our necks
in zero hurricanes.

O my land,
I see you as a woman in heat,
a bridge of lust.

The pharaohs take you when they choose,
and the very sand applauds them.
Through the clay of my eyeshells,
I see what any man can see:
libations at the graves of children,
incense for holy men,
tombstones of black marble,
fields scattered with skeletons,
vultures,
mushy corpses with the names of heroes.

Thus we advance,
chests to the sea,
grieving for yesterday.
Our words inherit nothing,
beget nothing.
We are islands.

From the abyss we smell ravens.
Our ships send out their pleas
to nothing but the moon's crescent
of despair that broods
a devil's spawn.
At riverfall, at the dead sea,
midnight dreams its festivals,
but sand and foam and locusts
are the only brides.

Thus we advance,
harvesting our caravans
in filth and tears,
bleeding the earth
with our own blood
until the green dam of the sea
alone
stops us.

2.

What god shall resurrect us
in his flesh?
After all, the iron cage is shrinking.
The hangman will not wait
though we wail from birth
in the name of these happy ruins.

What narrow yesterdays,
what stale and shriveled years . . .
Even storms come begging
when the sky matches the gray
of the sand,
leaving us stalled between seasons,
barricaded by what we see,

marching under clouds that move
like mules and cannon.
The dust of graveyards blinds us
until our eyes rhyme
with ash.
No lashes fringe the sun.
No brows can shade the day,
and life comes moment by moment
as it comes to the poor only.
Shadowed by ice and sand,
we live.

And so live all men.

All men . . . mere scraps from everywhere,
fresh baits of arsenic.
Under their sky what green can sprout?

All men . . . choked by ashes,
crushed by the rocks of silence,
mounted by empire builders,
paraded in arenas for their sport,
so many footstools,
so many banners . . .
No one whispers in Barada or the Euphrates.
Nothing breeds or stirs.
O my dry and silent land,
who left you like a fossil?
On the map you're virile,
rich with wheat, oil, ports,
countercolored by migrations.
Shall a new race grow in the poppy fields?
Shall fresh winds rearrange the sand?

Let the rain come.
Let rain wash us in our ruins,
wash the corpses, wash our history.
Let the poems strangled on our lips
be swept away like rocks in the street.
Let us attend to cows, doves, flowers, gods.
Let sounds return
to this land of starving frogs.
Let bread be brought by locusts
and the banished ants . . .

My words becomes a spear in flight.
Unopposable as truth,
my spear returns to strike me
dead.

    3.

Braid your hair, my boys, with greener leaves.
We still have verse among us.
We have the sea.
We have our dreams.
"To the steppes of China
we bequeath our neighing horses,
and to Georgia, our spears.
We'll build a house of gold
from here to the Himalayas.
We'll sail our flags in Samarkand.
We'll tread the treasured mosses
of the earth.
We'll bless our blood with roses.
We'll wash the day of stains
and walk on stones as we would walk on silk.

"This is the only way.
For this we'll lie with lightning
and anoint the mildewed earth
until the cries of birth
resound, resound, resound.

"Nothing can stop us.
Remember,
we are greener than the sea,
younger than time.
The sun and the day are dice
between our fingers."

Under the exile's moon
tremble the first wings.
Boats begin to drift
on a dead sea, and siroccos
rustle the gates of the city.
Tomorrow the gates shall open.
We'll burn the locusts in the desert,
span the abyss
and stand on the porch
of a world to be.

"Darkness,
darkness of the sea,
be filled with the leopard's joy.
Help us to sacrifice,
name us anew.
The eagle of the future waits,
and there are answers in its eyes.

"Darkness,
darkness of the sea,
ignore this feast of corpses.
Bring the earth to blossom
with your winds.
Banish plague and teach the very rocks
to dance and love."

The goddess of the sand prostrates herself.
Under brichthorn
the spring rises like clocynth from the lips
or life from the sea.
We leave the captive city
where every lantern is a church
and every bee more sacred than a nun.

4.
"Where is your home?
Which country?
Which camp without a name?"

"My country is abandoned.
My soul has left me.
I have no home."

When pharaohs ruled and men were cannibals,
the words of poets died.
While pharaohs rule,
I take my books and go,
living in the shade of my heart,
weaving from my verse's silk
a new heaven.

The sea cleanses our wounds
and makes of wounds the salt's kin . . .
The white sea,
the daily Euphrates,
the Orontes in its cradle,
the Barada—
I have tasted them all,
and none could slake me.
Yet I learned their love,
and my despair deserved such waters.

Though desperate, I still hate death.
Though lost, I seek my way
through all the lies and doubts
that are the crust and quicksand
of the earth.

Give me the exile's sail,
the pilgrim's face.
I turn my back on jails and holocausts.
I leave the dead to death.

And I go,
keeping my endless sorrows,
my distance from the stars,
my pilgrimage,
my girl
and my verses.
I go with the sweat
of exile on my forehead
and with a lost poem
sleeping in my eyes.
I go,
dreaming of those buried

in orchards and vineyards,
and I remember those I love,
those few.
When the sea rages my blood
and the wind kisses my love's hair,
I remember my mother,
and I weave in memory for her
a mat of straw
where she can sit and weep.

Amen to the age of flies.

Because the earth survives beneath my feet,
the pale god of my despair rejoices.
A new voice speaks my words.
My poems bloom naked as roses.

Find me some paper,
some ink.
Despair is still my star,
and evil is always being born.
Silence rises on the sand.
There are hearts to touch.
Some ink . . .
Some paper . . .

"Where is your home?
What camp without a name?"

"My country is abandoned.
My soul has left me.
I have no home."

Phoenix,
when the flames enfolded you,
what pen were you holding?
What feathers sprouted
when your old ones burned?
Buried in your own ashes,
what world did you confront,
what robe did you don,
what color did you choose?

Tell me.
Tell me what silence follows
the final silence
spun from the very fall of the sun?
What is it, phoenix?
Give me a word,
a sign.

Your banishment and mine
are one.
Your banishment and mine
and the banishment of heroes
are one.
Your banishment and mine
and the banishment of heroes
and the banishment of love and glory
are one.

What is it we love or fear
but shadows of ourselves?
When I recall your suffering,
my phoenix,
I forget my own.
No mother held you
when you left
until you burned for breath.
No father blessed your exile

in his heart
before you saw it born
in flame with each horizon.
I've left.
I've left my mother.
I've left my mother
on a mat of straw
to grieve my going.
Astray, I swallow dust.
I, who learned love
from my father's eyes,
have left my father's house
to be the prodigal.

I am a hunted bird.
I steal my bread.
All I see is desolation.
Pursued by falcons,
my small wings lose their feathers,
feather by feather.

"They say my song is strange
because it has no echo.
They say my song is strange
because I never dreamed
myself awake on silks.
They say I disbelieved the prophesies,
and it was true,
and it is still and always true."

My phoenix,
I learn with you
the banishment that murders me
in ruins and the sheerest voids.
I break from jail
to seek the man I keep becoming.
I leave the gate ajar,
the chain empty,

and the darkness of my cell
devours me like eyes in shadow.

Though banished,
I love all those who banished me,
who crowned my brow with chains
and waited to betray me.
I see my childhood
like an isolated Baalbek
with its longing pillars,
and I burn.
Horizon by horizon,
I am born to the chants of the sun.

My new wings grow
like yours, my phoenix.
Phoenix, we are born for death,
and death in life
deserves its springs and harvests,
its rivering Jesus,
its passion with the vineyard
and the mount.
But it is not all solitude
and echoes from the grave.

Phoenix, I remember one
who perished on a cross—
extinguished.
He burned in pools of cherry
like fire within fire
extinguished.
Yet from the dark of the ashes
he glows.

His wings are numbered
with the flowers of our land,
with all the days of all the years,
with pebbles and the merest stones.

Like you, my phoenix,
he survived our hunger,
and his mercy feeds us.

Dying with his wings outspread,
he gathered all who buried
him in ashes
and became, like you,
the spring and fire of our agony.

Go now, my sweet bird,
show me the road I'll follow.

1.

Picture the earth as a pear
or breast.
Between such fruits and death
survives an engineering trick:
New York.
Call it a city on four legs
heading for murder
while the drowned already moan
in the distance.
New York is a woman
holding, according to history,
a rag called liberty with one hand
and strangling the earth with the other.
New York
is damp asphalt
with a surface like a closed window.
I said: "Whitman can open it."
I say his password now,
but the absent god hears nothing.
Out of his stopped mouth
answer wretches, blacks and thugs.
I said: "The Brooklyn Bridge!"
But now it bridges Whitman and Wall Street,
a link between leaves of grass and the paper leaves
of dollar bills.
New York is Harlem.
What hangman is coming?
Will his coffin be as long as the Hudson?
Will this be the season of tears and weariness—
when pain is born of the sun,
and daylight pierces us
with its blue, yellow, rose and jasmine spears?

[57]

Wounds appear like clefts
between a thigh and a thigh.
Did the vulture visit you?
Did you hear the rattle of death,
feel the rope,
survive the necktwining sadness in your blood?
New York is Madison and Park Avenues and Harlem.
It is laziness that looks like work
and work that looks like laziness.
Hearts are sponges.
Hands are swollen reeds.
Out of an empire state of dirt and garbage
rises the stink of history.
Shall I prophesy that heads, not eyes, are blind,
that tongues, not words, are sterile?
New York is Wall Street and streets
named after numbers.
Call it Medusa,
a market for slaves
where people grow as plants grow
in glass gardens,
infiltrating like dust the fabric of space.
They are circling victims
already encircled.
Their day is a black drum
at the sun's funeral.

    2.

Here on the moss on the rocks of the earth
I stand unseen
except by blacks and birds about to be killed.
Even a plant in a red vase can follow the sun
but not I, the foreigner.
I learn of rats in my Beirut
or in a White House.

The rats are armed with paper.
They nibble at human flesh.
Or are they pigs in the orchards of language
who stamp on poetry?
In Pittsburgh, Baltimore, Cambridge,
Ann Arbor, Manhattan, the United Nations
Princeton and Philadelphia,
I saw the Arab map.
It resembled a mare shuffling on,
dragging its history like saddlebags,
nearing its tomb and the pitch of hell,
discovering the chemistry of Kirkukzahran and Afro-Asia.
But here a third war is being prepared
with a first, second, third and fourth
intelligence bureau created just in case.
Over there, a jazz festival.
In that house, a man with nothing but ink to his name.
In this tree, a single bird, singing.
Let us be frank and admit
that space is measured by walls or cages,
that time is clocked by ropes or whips,
that the system for building a world
begins with a brother's murder,
that the sun and moon are nothing
but a sultan's coins.
I saw names in Arabic.
Gigantic as the earth they were,
illuminated like an eye of ultimate compassion
but lagging like a wayward planet without a past
and slowing to a stop.

Here
on the moss on the rock of the earth
I know and say what I know.
I remember a plant called life.
I remember my land as I remember death,

a robe of wind
a face that murders me for no reason
or an eye that shuns the light
Against you, my country,
I still create to make you change
I stumble into hell and scream
while poisonous drops revive my memory of you.
New York, you will find in my land
a bed and silence,
a chair, a head,
the sale of day and night,
the stone of Mecca
and the waters of the Tigris.
In spite of all this,
you pant in Palestine and Hanoi.
East and west
you contend with people
whose only history is fire.
Since John the Baptist
each of us carries on a plate his cut head
and waits to be born again.

3

Let statues of liberty crumble.
Out of corpses now sprout nails
in the manner of flowers.
An eastern wind uproots tents and skyscrapers
with its wings.
In the west a second alphabet is born,
and the sun's mother is a tree in Jerusalem
I write in flames.
I start fresh, mixing and defining.
New York,
you are a mannikin suspended in a hammock,
swinging from void to void.
Ceilings crumble.

Your words are sins of a fall.
Shovels and hatchets are the ways you move.
Right and left,
people, hunger for love, sight, sound, smell
and change itself
to ransom them from time
and save whatever life remains.
Sex, poetry, morals, thirst, speech and silence
locked doors, all.
If I seduce Beirut or a sister capital,
she springs from bed,
lets memory be damned
and comes to me.
She lets me swing her from my poems.
Let doors be smashed by hatchets.
Let windows flaunt their flowers.
Let locks be burned.
So, I seduce Beirut.
Some say that words are dead,
that action is everything.
But I tell you that only their words are dead.
Their tongues have traded speech for pantomime.
But the world?
I tell you to remember its fire.
Write.
Don't mimic.
From the oceans to the gulf
I hear no tongues.
I read no words . . .
only sounds.
I see no igniter of fires.
The word, the lightest of things,
is everything.
Action is once.
The word is forever.

From word to hand to paper . . .
From hand and paper into dreams . . .
Thus I discover you, my fire, my capital,
my poetry.
I seduce Beirut.
I exchange identities with her.
We flee like beams and wonder who shall know
or who shall tell of us.
But Phantoms are as real
as oil flowing to its destination.
God and Mao were right: "Armies are an important
factor in war, but they are not decisive."
Men, not armies, are.
Why talk of final triumph, final defeat?
Neither exists.
Over and over I said such proverbs to myself
as an Arab would on Wall Street
where gold rivers converged on their sources.
Among them I saw Arab rivers
bearing human remnants, victims and gifts
to their idol and master.
Interspersed with the victims
cascaded sailors laughing down the Chrysler Building
to their sources.

Such visions ignite me.
Meanwhile, we live in a black upheaval
while our lungs fill with history's winds.
We rise above eyes that have been blinded
and bury ourselves in tombs against despair.
We go with blacks to greet the coming sun.

4.

New York,
you are a woman standing in the wind's archways,
a figure remote as an atom,
a mere dot in the numbered sky,
one thigh in the clouds, the other in water.
Tell me the name of your star.
A battle between grass and computers is coming.
The whole century is hemorrhaging.
Its head adds disaster to disaster.
Its waist is Asia.
Its legs belong to nothing . . .
I know you, O body, swimming in the musk of poppies.
You bare one nipple and its twin to me.
I look at you and dream of snow.
I look at you and wait for autumn.

Your snow is the bearer of night.
Your night bears souls away like dead bats.
You are a tomb.
Each of your days digs its own grave.
You bring me black bread on a black dish
and tell me fables of the White House.
First, dogs are handcuffed
while cats give birth to helmets and chains.
On narrow streets supported by the backs of rats,
white guards multiply like mushrooms.
Second, a woman follows a saddled dog
who moves like a king.
The town resembles an army in tears.
Out of the heaped, covered bodies of old and young,
bullets grow with the innocence of plants.
But who is knocking at the gates of the town?

[63]

Third, at Bedford-Stuyvesant
people are storied on people.
Time weaves their faces.
Refusals are children's meals,
and the meals of rats are children—
death-feasts for the trinity
of tax-collectors, policemen, judges.

Fourth, in Harlem the black hates the Jew.
In Harlem the black also hates the Arab
for he remembers slavery
On Broadway the walkers pass
like invertebrates embalmed
in alcohol and drugs.
In Harlem or on Broadway
a festival of chains and sticks
makes force the seed of time.
One shot: ten pigeons.
Boxed eyes quiver in red snow.
Time is a crutch.
Old blacks and infant blacks
falter
and fall.

    5.
Harlem,
Is it I am not a stranger.
I know your rancor.
I know how it tastes.
When you are starving,
thunder is the only answer.
When you are chained,
you yearn for havoc.
I watch the hidden fire advance
by hose and mask,
squelching denial and erasing footsteps like the wind.

Harlem,
time is dying, and you are the hour.
Your cries are bursting volcanoes.
Your people disappear like bread into a mouth.
But you shall erase New York.
You shall take it by storm
and blow it like a leaf away.
New York is IBM and the subway
emerging from mud and crime
and going to mud and crime.
New York is a hole in the world's pouch
for madness to gush in torrents.
Harlem, New York is dying, and you are the hour.

6.

Between Harlem and Lincoln Center
I walk like a lost number in a desert
streaked by the teeth of a black dawn.
No snow, no wind.
Hidden, I follow a shadow
which carries a bow that targets space.
It moves by faces that are not faces
but wounds,
by figures that are not figures
but dried flowers.
Is it a woman's shadow or a man's?
Earth-summoned, a deer passes.
Moon-summoned, a bird rises.
I feel them hurrying to witness the resurrection
of the Indian past
in Palestine and her sister countries.

Is space merely a pathway for bullets?
Is earth's purpose only to screen the dead?

I am an atom spinning on a beam
and aimed at the horizon.
It crosses my mind to doubt the roundness of the earth.

But home is still Mirene's daughter, Yara.
The earth is bounded by Yara and my daughter, Ninar.
Can I parenthesize New York?
Its avenues support my feet.
Its sky is a lake where my doubts and visions swim.
The Hudson flutters first like a crow
disguised as a nightingale.
Dawn advances, wounded and moaning.
I call the night.
It has left its bed and yielded to the sidewalk.
I see it hiding under a blanket thinner than the wind.
Again and again I cry.
New York stays stunned as a frog
in a waterless basin.

Abraham Lincoln,
New York is leaning on its crutches
and hobbling through memory's garden
of counterfeit flowers.
I face you now in your marble shrine in Washington,
having seen your twin in Harlem,
and wonder when your revolution will begin.
I want to set you free from white marble,
from presidencies,
from watchdogs and hunting dogs.
I want you to read
what I, Ali, son of Mohammed,
friend of the black man,
have read in the horizons of Marx, Lenin, Mao
and Niffari, that divine madman.
Niffari made the earth transparent
and learned to dwell between language and vision.
Lincoln, I want you to read
what Ho wanted to read
and Urwa, Ibn-al-Ward:
"I divide my body in many bodies."

Urwa never knew Baghdad
and probably refused Damascus.
He stayed in the desert
until he was strong enough to shoulder death.
He left to the lovers of the future
that part of the sun that was soaked
in the blood of the deer he used to call his love.
He agreed that the horizon was his final home.

Lincoln,
New York is a mirror reflecting Washington.
And Washington reflects the president
and the cries of this world.
Let the weepers stand and dance.
There is still time, still a role for them.
I fall in love with their dance,
see it change into a bird,
then a deluge.
"The world needs a deluge,"
I said and wept instead of rage.
How shall I convince Al-Murrah of Abi-al-Ala?
The prophet's birthplace always denies him.
How shall I convince the plains of the Euphrates
of the Euphrates?
How can I exchange helmets for wheat?
One needs courage to ask the prophet's questions.
Even while I say this
I see a cloud necklaced with fire.
I see people melting like tears.

7.

New York,
I corner you with words.
I grasp you, squeeze you,
write and erase you.
In hot and cold and in between,
awake, asleep or in between,

I stand above you and sigh.
I pass ahead of you
and warn you to stay behind.
I crush you with my eyes—
you who are crushed with fear.
I try to rule your streets
or lie between your thighs
and make you into something new
or wash you so I can re-name you.
I used to see no difference
between a tree and a man—
one with a crown of branches,
the other crowned with his branching nerves.
Now I cannot separate pebbles from cars,
shoes from helmets,
bread from tin.
In spite of this New York is not nonsense.
After all, it is two words.
But when I write the letters of Damascus,
I mimic nonsense.
I create nothing.
Damascus—a sound, something of the wind.
Years back, she stepped out of my pages
and has not returned.
Time guards the threshold
and wonders when or if she will return.
The same is true of Beirut, Cairo, Baghdad—
so much nonsense floating like dust in sunrays.
One sun,
two suns,
three, a hundred . . .
A man awakens every day from reassurance
to anxiety.
He leaves a wife and children for a rifle.
One sun,
two suns,
three, a hundred . . .

He returns like used thread discarded in a corner.
He sits in a cafe.
The cafe fills with stones and dolls called men,
or are they really frogs who speak their filth
and foul their chairs?
How can a man revolt when his brain is bloody,
and his blood enslaved?
I ask you, how?
Tell me, you who warn me to ignore science
and specialize in the chemistry of the Arabs.

8.

The house of Mrs. Brewing, a Greek woman in New York,
   a page from the book of the eastern Mediterranean.
   Mirene, Nimat Allah, Yves Bonnefoy . . . And I am like
   someone lost who is saying what cannot be said. Cairo
   seems scattered between us, a rose indifferent to time.
   Alexandria merges with the voices of Cavafy and Seferis.
   "This is a byzantine ikon," she says and the moment
   gives her lips a red scent. Time seems to stop; the snow
   suspends itself. (Midnight, April 6, 1971).

I wake up in the morning, shortly before the time I must
   leave, shouting: "New York!

"You mold children like snow-men, and you make a cake
   of our era! Your voice is oxide, a poison more powerful
   than any alchemy. Your name is insomnia, suffocation.
   Central Park offers its victims a feast, but under its trees
   are the ghosts of cadavers and daggers. Only bare
   branches are left to the winds, and a blocked road con-
   fronts the traveler."

I wake up in the morning, shouting, "Nixon, how many
    children have you killed today?"
        "This question is not interesting." (Calley)
        "It is true that there is a problem here. But is it not
    also true that we reduce the ranks of the enemy this way?"
    (An American general)

How shall I give the heart of New York a new dimension?
    Is the heart able to create new contours for itself?

New York—the General Motors of Death:
        "We shall replace people with fire." (McNamara)
        "They will dry up the sea where the insurgents swim."
        "They transform the earth into a desert and call it
    peace." (Tacitus)

I rise in the morning and awaken Whitman.

    9.
Walt Whitman,
I see letters careening toward you
down the streets of Manhattan.
Each letter carries cats and dogs.
To cats and dogs the twenty-first century!
To people, extermination in this
the American century.

Whitman,
I did not see you in all Manhattan.
The moon was an orangeskin chucked from a window;
the sun, an orange neon.

Out of Harlem shot one of the black roads of the moon,
but where was it going?
A light follows it still, illuminating the asphalt
all the way to Greenwich Village,
that other Latin Quarter.
Whitman,
a clock announces time to New York
like garbage thrown to a woman
who is nine parts ashes.
A clock announces time
where Pavlov experiments with people
in the system of New York.
A clock announces time
while a letter comes from the east
written in a child's blood.
I scan it until the child's doll
becomes a cannon or a rifle.
Corpses in their streets make sisters
of Hanoi, Jerusalem and Cairo.
Whitman,
a clock announces time
while I see what you never saw
and know what you could never know.
I move like someone screened
from neighbors who themselves are cancers
in an ocean of a million islands.
Each one is a column with two hands,
two legs and a broken head.
And you, Walt Whitman,
stay exiled like an immigrant.
Have you become a bird unknown in the American sky?
Whitman,
let our turn be now.
Let's make a ladder with our visions,
weave a common pillow with our footsteps.

Shall we be patient?
Man dies but still outlasts his monuments.
Let our turn be now.
I expect the Volga to flow between Manhattan and Queens
I expect the Huang Ho to replace the Hudson.
Are you astonished?
Did the Orontes not dilute the Tiber?
Let our turn be now.
I hear an earthquake and war.
Wall Street and Harlem are colliding
like thunder and leaves,
like dust and dynamite.
But shells reveal themselves when the waves pass.
The tree remembers it is a tree.
Mankind attends to its wounds.
The sun changes its mask
and mourns with its darker eye.
Let our turn be now.
We can outrun speeding wheels,
crush atoms,
outswim computers,
capture a plain and sparkling country
from the birds.
Let our turn be now.
Our book is on the rise,
and it is not mere print
but a prophecy that grows and grows,
a beginning of a wise madness,
the clearing up that follows a rain,
the sun's inheritance.
Let our turn be now.
New York is a rock thrown at the world's brow.
Its voice is in my clothes and yours.
Its charcoal dyes your limbs and mine.
I see what waits us at the end,
but how can I persuade the clock

to spare me until it comes.
Let our turn be now.
Let us be the executioners.
Let time keep floating on the sea of that equation:
New York plus New York equal a funeral.
New York minus New York equal the sun.

10.

When I was eighteen in the eighties,
Beirut did not hear me.
Under my clothes under my skin is a corpse.
A corpse is what sleeps like an endless book.
It does not inhabit the past and syntax of the body.
A corpse reads the earth in stones, not rivers.
(Excuse me, but I often like proverbial wisdom.
After all, if you are not passionate,
You are already a corpse.)
I say now and again
that my poems are trees
where nothing but a single trunk
unites branch with branch and leaf with leaf.
I say now and again
that poetry is the rose of all winds—
not wind only, but tempests,
not one circling, but orbits, orbits.
Thus I break rules and create rules
second by second.
I go away but never exit.

In Berkeley or Beirut or other hives,
what preparations!
Between a face transfigured by marijuana at midnight
and a face that IBM emblazons on the cold sun,
I let the angry river of Lebanon flow,
Gibran on one shore
and Adonis on the other.
So I left New York as I might leave a bed,

the woman in it like a stifled star,
the bed shattering.
I moved between a clutch of trees
that moaned the wind.
I passed a cross without a memory of thorns.

Now before the bearer of the first water
that wounds Descartes or Aristotle,
I share myself between my home in Ashrafiah
and the Ras-Beirut Bookshop,
between my students at Zahrat-al-Ahssan
and the Hayek Press.
My writings become a palm tree;
the tree, a dove.

For a thousand and one nights
Leyla and Buthaina stay unfound.
Going from stone to stone, Jameel pursues his destiny,
forever searching,
forever unfulfilled
And no one discovers Kaiss.*

Still
I salute the dusk flowers
and the flowers of the sand.
Beirut,
I still salute you.

* Leyla, Buthaina, Jameel and Kaiss are legendary figures from Arabic tales of unre-
quited love.

TRANSFORMATIONS OF THE LOVER

"Women are your garments, and you are theirs."
The Koran
"The body is the dome of the soul."
St. Gregoire Palamas

1.

. . . Faster than the air I ran
beneath the jailing sky until I disappeared in darkness.
The wind kept calling me by name.
I heard the echo of an old man's voice:
"You will discover a mountain filled with your necessities.
It will protect you and grant you victory."
Then I heard a voice from within the mountain:
"Pull aside the curtain and enter."
I entered the mountain as through a window . . .
A hand beckoned me toward an ageless place
that glowed in the light.
A bed awaited me there, and on it lay an image
with breasts and thighs and all the rest.

I awoke beside a woman
who became my other nature,
and that nature flowered suddenly like poppies or plants.
Male and female it flowered.

My body started to prepare itself for something
like the fall of planets.

2.

Her body grew north, south, east, west.
It grew upward to new depths.
Like a spring she welcomed me,
and like a tree she surrendered to me.

Suspended in my dream,
I kept imagining my dream into the world,
inventing secrecies to fill the flaws of all my days.
I burned against her like an ember.

My lips and fingers were pens on her flesh.
I memorized her in every alphabet
and memorized my memories until they multiplied.

My sighs were clouds that made their own horizons.
I wove her a robe from the sun.
The light of midnight traveled me to her.

I hid in the folds of her robe.
We learned the world together.
At the sound of doorbells we disappeared.
I sat beside her while she read.
I slept like tears between the lashes of her eyes.
Suddenly I lost sight of her.
She was everywhere I'd never been.
Her garments and her seasons
became my pathway to her.

We knifed our names it treetrunks.
We rolled downhill like stones.
We sang with trees,
and the earth was like the fruit of love for us.

Clouds were our friends.
Stonehouses understood us.
The memory of daylight disappeared behind us.

In Qasyun she emerged like incense,
and I swayed in the scent
of her shy and intimate taste.

   3.
We woke to the bitter threads of dawn
that changed into people and mosses from the sea.

Our eyelids tightened like knots.
The sunlight striped and bannered our bodies
before it flamed across our pillows.

Our eyelids tightened into harder knots.

The dawn ordered the night to awaken.

My body was a vessel I shared with her.
I discovered with the map of sex a new earth,
and I advanced toward it.

I disguised my path with riddles and signs
that vaporized in my delirium like tattoos of fire.
I was a wave advancing toward her shore.
Her back was a continent, and the world's compass
hid beneath her breasts.

I enclosed her as if I were the branches of a tree.
We felt between us a power
like the wings of a thousand eagles.
I listened to her at passion's brink . . .
the sigh of her waist, the surge of her hips.

Overcome, I entered the desert of panic
and whispered her name.
I descended lower and lower
until I reached her narrower world
where fire and tears were one and the same.

I watched the wonder of all I saw
until I was drunk with seeing.
The lord of the flesh spoke to me.

Three hundred and sixty-five days encircled me.
I made homes of every day, made beds in every home
and slept in every bed.

[77]

(When love's hour begins,
the moon and the sun are the same.)

She bore me like a river.
I heard another language
that turned into gardens, stones, waves, more waves
and flowers with supernatural thorns
as the lord of the flesh commanded.

"My beloved, whose body I have scriptured with love's pen,
do what you will with me.
Stop and speak
until you sunder me and free my treasures.

If I am static as the stars, re-order me.
If I am higher than the clouds
or lower than a spring on any mountain's peak
remain beneath me.

I see your face in every other face.
You are the sun that travels neither east nor west.
You neither wake nor sleep.
You are my resurrection and my fall.
You seam my sorrows.
You let my meteoring verses be the death of thorns.
You let me hold like wind the very planets in my hand
until they're purified and lost
No wonder I assault you with my heart
and know you, pore by pore.
Why?
Because your whispering invites me."

In bed or on the ground itself
we planted saplings of the flesh.
We hid in conversation long enough
to make a new epiphany.

Her body was mine, and mine was hers.
We were transformed into each other.
The architecture of our joints, the pulse in the limbs,
the pure geometry of muscles
and the glory of the act that bound us, navel to navel,
contractions of the flesh, descent and ascent,
plateaus and flights and waves,
her waist like a floor of stars and half-stars
and volcanoes and embers
and the waterfalls of twin desires . . .

Afterward, we hid like twins in shadow
where the galaxy of sex was king.
We lay transformed.
Her breasts were night and day to me.
Standing, we felt between us an opening of frontiers.
No longer captives of ourselves,
we started the clock of the sun we stopped together.
We let it summon fruit and flowers with its light.

We seemed more quietly alive.
We saw a new earth blossoming with trees
planted by the lord of the flesh.

    4.
In the sea of love or on the winds of love and fate
we were enthroned like a living book of flesh
on the world's weight.

Our each body was a water-carried dome
borne toward the seventh heaven . . .

"Beloved, what do you see?"

"I see a knight who says
that nothing I desire cannot be mine.
We sowed wheat seeds and told them to grow,

and they grew and were harvested.
We said, 'Be husked.'
And they were husked.
We said, 'Be ground.'
And they were ground.
We said, 'Be baked.'
And they were baked.
And when we saw that everything we wanted we received,
we feared and awoke,
and we shared the same pillow."
"And you, my lover, what did you see?"

"Children before a wind ablaze with meteors."

"What else?"

"A slope that moved and changed into a pregnant gazelle."

"What else?"

"The two of us together on a ship.
We embraced, and the ship shattered.
We clung to a spar that saved us.
Lying on it, you gave birth.
You said, 'I'm thirsty.'
I knew that I could give you nothing but the sea to drink.
Then I saw a spirit in the sky who offered me
a flask.
After you drank, I drank as well,
and the water was honey."

The spirit vanished, saying, 'I will leave love
to you and return to the kingdom of the air.'

My body turned into a new horizon,
and my limbs were palm trees.

You give me your fruit, beloved.
I am plucked alert beneath your breast.
You are myrtle and water to me.
Your fruits are wounds and roads at once.
I enter you.
You sheathe me.
I dwell in you as in a sea.
Your body is a wave.
Your body is April itself, and every part
of you becomes a dove that speaks my name.

You hold my limbs in yours until I'm drunk
as any sufferer.
I grow into your east and west
and taste the dust of the grave.
I am your kingdom's plunderer and saviour.
I tremble and dare.
I call upon what grows.
I pray to the wilderness . . .
I feel the courage of panthers
and the loneliness of eagles."

Torn, I fell into caverns
filled with creatures without faces.
Surrounded by them, I knelt there.

No longer myself, bewildered,
I spurned the earth and kept what I'd become.
The rest was an abyss
that opened and closed on me.

I gossiped with an angel, listened to waves,
crossed bridges to the bottom of the world
and then returned, my limbs intact,
my shattered heart in my hands.
Out of this dream I heard her summon me,
"Where were you, my love?

You took so long to enter the tent of my body,
to be its spine and moorings.
Why did you take so long, my love?"

The child-god beneath my garments screamed for love.
He was tired of bearing the burden of roads
His lamps were trees.
He ruled the bells and towers of the air.
His love was like the wind of creation,
reaching beyond all brinks
until it turned into the sky, the sky, the sky.

I arrived beyond the sea,
beyond sea-charmed trees, beyond mountains
to find her body like a city.
From the base of her neck
to the arch of her eyelids
her beauty made a slave of me.
She had the grace of wild birds,
and love gloried in her pulse.

Doors became transparent.
Windows raised themselves.
Closets glittered like gardens or piazzas.

"Do you remember, my beautiful,
how our home bloomed in orchards of olives and figs,
how the spring slept beside it
like the apple of your eye?

Do you remember, my beautiful,
how the branches fluttered with butterflies,
and every night was a new beginning on earth?

Every night you embraced me,
and I touched the smooth wilderness
between your breasts.

[82]

I shall leave a history of thunder,
of plains ploughed by exile,
of caravans in passage,
of islands and inkpots.
I shall never halt until death halts me.

At night
when I erect my tent,
I quiver as we touch.
Each quiver's a country,
and the road to every country beckons me.
We bow, we meet, we pass or sit opposite each other.
You are my garments, and I am yours.
Our muscles tense.
Our skins taste like a violent sea
that sails us in its welcome.

We hear beds moaning like lovers.
We feel that we are touching death itself.
We turn and arch.
Love's our saviour.
It satisfies as water satisfies the thirsty.

Let there be weddings!
A magic brighter than the sun illuminates us.
The spring we swim in purifies us.

Let there be weddings!
We avenge death with the sacrifice of ourselves.
In love or out of love, awake or asleep,
we serve the all-seeing god of darkness.

Let there be weddings!
Each time we lose ourselves in sex,
we face a dream of cities
revolving like globes beneath our eyelids.
Love begets love as distance begets distance
and you are that love, that distance, my beloved.

[83]

When you desired me, you let me create you.
When I wanted you, you were there for me like water.
Your pulse became my pulse.
I painted your breasts with words,
and we drowned in love's waters.

In the city of ourselves
we live like love's parishioners.

Each day's an open book
that we write with our eyes.

You are a secret beyond dreams.
You are love beyond the heart itself,
and we take new names each time we waken.

You are a lake.
I am a willowtrunk spearing your earth.
I cast anchor at your shore.
Your waist is my anchorage.
You are all women in one, all lovers in one.

What tides await us at the gulf?
I am a closed shell, and you are my pearl.
Your face is all the guide I need.

I bare day's other face.
I see the opposite of night.
I shout at the sea until it shatters like a reed.
I say to thunder, 'Listen!
Is love the only place unvisited by death?
Are we the perishers still capable of knowing love?
Death, give me a name to call you by!'

A space divides me from myself
where death and love await me.
Flesh is my baptism.
From the depth of all that perishes, I sing of love . . .' "

5.

"Why did you marry me?"

"I was just walking with nothing of my own,
nowhere to rest.
I slept and awoke,
and you were lying on my pillow.
I thought of Eve and Adam's rib . . .
I dreamed that clouds rose before me.
A voice said, 'Choose whatever you want'
And I chose a stormcloud, and we both drank from it.
I said, 'Let my flesh shrink and stretch,
appear and disappear.
My clothes abandoned me, and darkness clothed me.
The world made its home within me and said,
'Descend deeply into darkness.'
So I entered darkness itself
and saw a stone, a light, sands and running water.
I met myself in you and said,
'I will never leave this darkness.'
But the sun betrayed me by illuminating everything."

"But how, how did you marry me?"

"My body came to you like the wind
colored by the earth itself.
Like planets of wind we loved."

6.

Yesterday I closed my door at the sight of the first star.
I pulled the curtains, and I entered her.

If I'm a sorcerer, my love's like incense.
If I'm a sorcerer, my love's a fire, an altar, an ember.
I turn into smoke.
I conjure up a sign to dazzle her.
Her loins conceal a wound that awes me

[85]

and holds my ultimate death
in a kingdom of towers and angels . . .

I see a naked man crushing hurricanes in ecstasy.
Baptized by waterfalls, he drops to his knees
and disappears.

I dreamed I washed the earth
until it glistened like a mirror.
I walled it with clouds and fenced it with fire.
I held it in my hands and domed it with tears.

"What final gift are you preparing for me?"

"I'll wrap you in wedding clothes, my beautiful,
and introduce you to the grave
so you will have no fear of death
or of the death of love.
I'll swim with you and give you death to drink.
I'll give you everything between the grave
and death's gratuities"

I said, "If only a woman could be transparent as the sky.
If only the world could be a stone named sex."

And I kept imagining that she was like a sea in space
until I fell in love with foam
and hid it in my eyes
and swore that waves would be my neighbor.

In her depths I drowned my sorrows.

Awake with me all night she whispers,
"You are my angel.
Beneath your skin an angel hides.

Let's plunge into the deep again, my love,
and leave to others
the height and breadth
of all the other kingdoms of the air."

WISHES

If I were water, I would pierce whatever's solid.
I would search beneath the soil.
I would live the fate of dew and clouds.

If I were a cloud,
I would pass above sheperds in spring
and be like a tent for lovers.

If I were a field, I would be a harvest.
I would understand like planted grain
how the seasons begin and continue.

If I were a candle,
I would experience the passing of time
in bread rising . . . in a tear.

I would restrain myself, and on my sky
would be inscribed words like *ash* and *charcoal*.
But because I am blood and flesh,

I love what I am and hate my love for it.
Is there another way I can create this world?

GILGAMESH

Between myself and the road before me—
sadness.
Did I die when my country began to shrink
and my desire overwhelmed me?
Were my words extinguished?
Shall I say now: "I am not myself."
Shall I say: "I have created ashes."

NEFFARI

The sun made me the same as trees,
as rivers, as the poor.
Ask the sun how it made me an exile.

It scattered me on the road,
letter by letter,
and the languages of exile
are not the sun's languages.

I have thus become a wanderer.
To be an exile is my identity.

THE BEGINNING OF NAMING

We have named every place
in the name of the sword
and have started to build

a moon from chalk,
forests from severed heads,
and the stars from a night of cadavers.

We have created a kingdom of mere things.

[88]

POLLEN

Sometimes the field sprouts nails,
so much does the field long for water.

*

The solitude of winter
and the passing of summer
are linked by the bridge of spring.

*

A voice is the dawn of language.

*

Dust is a body
which does not dance
except with the wind.

POLLEN II

Nature does not age.

*

I'm grateful to time
which bears me in its arms
and erases every road I've taken.

*

Open your arms.
I would like to see
my memory
trembling between them.

ABU NUWAS

The charm of language—the blood of words—
and the sky a thoroughfare.
And I? A mere passerby
who interrupts the sky.

THE BEGINNING OF THE ROAD

He read each day like a book
and saw the world as a lantern
in the night of his fury.
He saw the horizon come to him
as a friend.
He read directions
in the faces of poetry and fire.

THE DESERT

Diary of Beirut under Siege, 1982

1.
The time of my life tells me:
"You do not belong here."
I answer frankly.
Granted, I don't belong.
I try my best to understand you,
but I am lost
like a shadow in a forest
of skulls.

2.
I'm standing now.
This wall is nothing but a fence.
Distance shrivels; a window fades.

Daylight is but a thread
I snip to stitch my way to darkness,
breath by breath.

3.

Everything I ever said of life and death
repeats itself in the silence
of the stone that pillows my head.

4.

Do I contradict myself? Absolutely.
Today I'm a plant.
Yesterday I was an element
between fire and water.
I was something to harvest.
Now I'm a rose, a burning coal.
I am sun and shadow,
but I'm not a god.
Do I contradict myself? Absolutely.

5.

The moon arms itself
with a cap of stone
to battle its shadows.

6.

The door of my house is sealed.
Darkness blankets me.
The moon offers me
its paltry alms of light.
I choke with gratitude,
but I cannot speak.

7.
Murder has transformed Beirut.
Rock is really bone.
Smoke is but the breath of human beings.

8.
We meet no more.
Denial and exile separate us.
Promises have died.
Space is irrelevant.
Death becomes our only point of contact.

9.
He locks the door,
not to seal in his happiness
but to free his sorrow.

10.
Bulletins:
a woman in love's been killed,
a boy kidnapped,
a policeman crushed against a wall.

11.
The future is already old,
so take everything
but this insanity with you.
Consider yourself a stranger
if you stay.

12.
People were found in sacks:
a head only in one sack,
a tongueless and headless corpse
in another,
in a third what once was a body,
the rest, nameless.

Have we gone mad?
Do not, please, report these things.

13.
You will soon see.
Say a name.
Paint a profile.
Offer your hand.
Walk like anybody.
Smile.
Speak of sadness.
You will see.
This is not your country any more.

14.
The time is coming when it will be mandatory
to hear and say nothing.
Oh, perhaps they'll let you whisper:
"Death, life, resurrection,
and peace be with you."

15.
He wears the uniform of holy war
and poses in the cloak of ideology.
He's really a merchant,
not dealing in clothes but in people.

16.
They dragged him to a trench and set him on fire.
He murdered no one.
He was a boy.
He was not . . .
He was a voice in space.
Now the air holds his memory.

17.
Night.
Trees seem like tears from heaven.
It's like an eclipse.
The city was a branch
broken by death,
and the people fled.

18.
You were not killed because you lived
in a body created by God.
You were killed because you were the future.

19.
The flower that lured the wind
to bear away its sweet scent
died yesterday.

20.
The sun rises no more.
It shrouds itself with straw
and vanishes.

21.
Death will come at night.
I will give him a cushion of roses.
I'm sick of all these dawns of dust.
I am tired of hearing people breathe.

22.
From the wine of the palm to the peace of the desert . . .
from the morning's hunger that slouches the shoulders
    of the refugees . . .
from the streets, trucks and soldiers in formation . . .
from the shadows of women and men . . .
from bombs that gorge on the blood of Muslims
    and unbelievers . . .

from armor that bleeds and sweats pus . . .
from the fields that hunger for wheat, for growth,
    for farmers . . .
from castles that shield our bodies and punish us
    with darkness . . .
from the myths of the dead that tell us what we know
    of life . . .
from words that kill each other and all who hear them . . .
from darkness, darkness, darkness,
I breathe and feel my life while I search
    for you, for myself, for everybody.
Between my face and these words written in blood,
I discover death.

23.

When trees bend, they say goodbye.
When flowers bloom, blaze and close,
    they say goodbye.
Young bodies that vanish in chaos say goodbye.
Papers that thirst for ink say goodbye.
The alphabets and poets say goodbye.
Finally the poem says goodbye.

24.

The airborne killer
circles the wounded city.
The wound is the fall of the city.
It shivers at the mention of its name—
its name now written in blood.
Everything changes around us.
Houses have no interiors.
Even I am not myself any longer.

25.

Bombs are mirrored in books
along with prophecies and ancient wisdom
and hidden places.

Memory is a needle
that stitches a carpet of words like threads
over the face of Beirut.

26.
Even the stars seem bloody.
A boy sees blood in every star
and whispers to his friends:
"The only holes left in the sky
are stars."

27.
Night and daylight are the same.
In the darkness of the heart
sunlight and candlelight are one and the same.

28.
It's wrong to expect the sun not to record
what's written in the fields
and what the seasons forgot.

29.
Night happens (these are papers he saved
      to write on, but the writing never came).
Night happens on a bed (the bed of a lover,
      but there is no lover).
Night happens without a sound in clouds of smoke.
Night happens while someone carries ants and rabbits
      in his hand.
Night happens while the walls shudder,
      and the curtains reveal everything.
Night happens, but no one listens (the stars are mute,
      and the last trees by the wall have
      forgotten what the wind said to them).
Night happens while the wind whispers at a window.
Night happens while lights try to shine,
      and a man lies naked.

Night happens, revealing through a window
    two women embracing.
Night happens, and the whimsical moon would complain
    if it could in the language of lovers.
Night happens while a man alone and without friends
    fills his glass from a pitcher of wine.
Night happens while a few spiders relax
    with other insects that used to be house pets,
    while lights burst upon us (is it the approach
    of angels, missiles or a surprise?),
    while our women returning from pilgrimage
    are surprisingly fatter and more flirtatious.
Night happens as if a woman's breasts were days,
    and nights the shadow between them.
Night happens on a sofa, a pillow, in an alley, anywhere.
Night happens while we hunger for wine, soup and bread
    and yet are blind to the night's hunger.
Night happens while we play for time with snails,
    with nameless doves from abroad,
    with insects that have never been identified
    in any biology book.
Night happens in thunder after thunder like a storm
    of angels charging on their horses.
Night happens while a man mumbles and fingers a glass.

30.

When the sun begins to set,
so many seagulls soar
that they became a cloth
that veils the sky.

31.

He wrote a poem that said, "I don't know where the road
    begins or how to bare my forehead to the sun."
He wrote a poem that said, "My future is a desert,
    and my blood, a mirage."
He wrote a poem that softened my hard shell.

[97]

He wrote a poem that ordered me to qualify
    by killing my brother.
He wrote a poem that prophesied a future
    no one expected
    nor even thought possible.
He wrote a poem that suspended language like a thief
    between truth and itself.
He wrote a poem that urged the moon to imitate a candle.
He wrote a poem that confused the face of the sun
    with the sky.
He wrote a poem that killed him.

32.

The cities shatter.
The earth is nothing but dust.
Only one thing can unify them—love.

33.

Should I mourn him now that he is dead?
What should I say?
Should I say that his life was a word,
    but only his death could give it meaning.
Or should I say the road to light
    starts in a dark wood.
Chaos.. . . . voices. . . .
I choose the entrance to a cave to shield me
while I pray.

34.

He fled the caravanserai,
refusing the flute and its temptations
for a life alone
where the scent of the withering rose
was all that drew him.

35

You will always be my friend
among what was or what remains in this rubble.
O light that guides the clouds . . .
O Lord whose goodness never sleeps . . .

(June 4, 1982–January 1, 1983)

1.

At the origin of the word "difficult" and the phenomena to which it refers in pre-Islamic Arab poetry, there are certain images that shed light on the relationship between the poem and its listeners. We climb a steep mountain; a rebellious camel refuses to be broken and ridden; the fruit we crave is inaccessible; a cloud is charged with thunder and lightning: all of these images resist ease and facility. When Arab listeners heard a "difficult" poetry, these were the images that came into their minds. Their natural inclination led them toward a poetry that evoked the opposite of these images, a poetry that could be assimilated without trouble or effort, a poetry like a light cloud, a straight and level path, a fruit within easy reach of the hand, a docile camel. The Arab demanded of the poem an easiness that would allow him to dominate it intellectually, to take possession of it with the cognitive tools at his disposal. He rejected any poem that did not correspond to this demand and qualified it as "difficult," a word that was usually pejorative. It was said that a "difficult" poet hewed stone while an "easy" poet dipped into the sea . . .

2.

This was the prevailing relationship between the poem and its listeners during the pre-Islamic period of oral poetry. The same relationship continued to prevail in the Islamic period, over the course of which it took on, with the advent of writing, a new dimension that could be described as ideological *avant la lettre*. Any discussion of Arab poetry must very precisely take into account the Muslim's attitude toward his language. Pagan before Islam, the Arabic language becomes divine through the Qur'anic Revelation but is not otherwise altered. Arabic is thus the matrix or mother of the Word of God and also of pre-Islamic poetry, pagan though it was. When this divine Revelation came to take the place of poetic inspiration, it claimed to be the sole source of knowledge, and banished poetry and poets from their kingdom. Poetry was no longer the word of truth, as the pre-Islamic poets had claimed it was. Never-theless—and this merits a separate study—Islam did not suppress poetry as a form and mode of expression. Rather, it nullified poet-ry's role and cognitive mission, endowing it with a new function: to celebrate and preach the truth introduced by the Qur'anic Reve-lation. Islam thus deprived poetry of its earliest characteristics—intuition and the power of revelation and made it into a media tool.

As a revealed religion, Islam unites words and actions. Hence its political tendency, manifested in its literature by the close ties be-tween poetry and the other forms of writing that serve the Islamic message, and also by the ostracism (marginalization, exclusion or interdiction) of anything that does not serve that message. We can perhaps detect the first seeds of the ideological use of art here. It should be noted that what rivaled and still rivals poetry in Arab society is not science or philosophy, but religion. For in its original, pre-Islamic sense, poetry is inspiration—which is to say prophecy—but without commandments, institutions or norms. However, start-ing with Islam—and this also deserves a separate study—poetry in Arab society has languished and withered precisely insofar as it has placed itself at the service of religiosity, proselytism and political and ideological commitments. The eighth-century critic Al-Asma'i alludes to this in a clairvoyant phrase: "Poetry is a misadventure that begins with Evil; as soon as it interferes with Good, it founders." So we can imagine the sort of adventure that poetry has lived—and still lives—within a "divine" language, in a society whose social, cultural and political structures are all founded on a Revelation expressed in that same language.

3.

As the Revelation was embodied in institutions that saw in poetry only a tool which could serve them, new relationships between poetry and its listeners were established in daily life. New ways of appreciating poetry also emerged, along with new values and crite-ria. The politico-religious institution exercised its power as a faith-ful guardian of the Qur'anic Revelation. It possessed the absolute certitude that the Revelation spoke and wrote Man and the uni-verse clearly, definitively and without error or imperfection. This certitude, in turn, demanded that the Muslim individual be formed around a faith in an absolute text, one which allowed no interrogation that might give rise to any doubt whatsoever.

Under such conditions, alienation is inevitable; the skeptical individual no longer has the right to be a member of the society. Because Islam—the last message sent by God to mankind—has placed the final seal on the Divine Word, successive words are incapable of bringing humankind anything new. A new message would imply that the Islamic message did not say everything, that it is imperfect. Therefore the human word must, on an emotional level, continually eulogize and celebrate that message: on an intellectual level, *a fortiori* it can only serve as explication.

Poetry, the most elevated form of expression, will henceforth be valued only for its obviousness. As a tool for instruction, poetry must cultivate the easiness that will best enable it to disseminate its message. And this easiness ultimately transforms poetry into an object of consumption. By appealing to poetic memory, poetry gives the illusion of joining the present to the past and of responding to people's real needs. But in the course of this process, it does not liberate; it anesthetizes, as if it were teaching the faithful to manufacture their prisons and their chains with their own desires, their own needs. This easiness turns Man toward the past; it is not an energy propelling him toward the future.

In part, this explains the dominance in the Arab mentality of what I call "pastism." In the context of this inquiry, pastism means the refusal and fear of the unusual. When it confronts a poetry that does not derive from what it already knows, this mentality first tries to grasp it by comparing it to the religio-linguistic heritage, to what is already known. The greater the disparity, the more the poetic production will be considered foreign and dangerous, a threat to the sacred patrimony. The important thing is to identify a clear and direct line connecting the present to the past.

4.

Thus poetry's final aim is to transmit the message it bears rather than to reveal the poet's self and his individual vision of human existence and the world. The value of the poem resides in its effi-

[103]

cacy and in the breadth of the satisfaction it can give. That being so, poetry comes to resemble all other institutions: it is marriage, not love; the arrival, not the adventure; the object, not the subject. Poetry becomes the promulgator of inherited values and the safeguard of their continuity. Linguistic production is envisioned as a kind of manual production, and poetic language as a mode of work. And like the product of the laborer's work, which is subject to exchange, the poem produced by the work of the linguistic laborer will also be a piece of merchandise that one can exchange ... The value of the poem therefore resides in its capacity to please and to attract.

We should note in passing that the modern media, at all levels, contribute to the ever-increasing superficiality and banality of the world. They reduce all writing, including poetry, to pieces of information among other pieces of information. In so doing, they negate writing and reading alike, and reinstitute a culture of the eye and the ear, which is no more than a form of illiteracy. Productivity takes the place of creativity; the producer is substituted for the creator.

Within Arab society, this universal state of things is translated by the movement toward Arab traditionalism. Particularly in regard to poetic writing, this traditionalism crystallizes the society's will to put the creator to death. The poetic work is held to be the reflection of the Revealed Text which has been handed down by God, the Prophet serving only as an intermediary. Since poetry derives from religion and from the community of believers, the poet, too, is no more than an intermediary.

This phenomenon is anchored in poetic and historic memory. The pre-Islamic Arabs spoke a poetry that began with a concrete situation, or rather with an event-word. The word was essentially linked to life, movement and work. It was originally carnal, and the poem was a kind of nourishment; it was judged by its savor. People expected poetry to grant them access to their present circumstances, to address their daily life, to bring them back to their realities. Poetry's faithfulness to reality was the principal criterion. The relationship of poetry to what people enjoyed or rejected was stronger than its relationship to the categories of beauty and ugliness. The relationship between word and thing was the primordial expression of a situation, and was therefore an ethical and not an aesthetic relationship.

This can explain the importance of conventions in Arab poetic writing, which is primarily constituted of rules and principles.

The idea of the beautiful appeared only when Arabs began to distance themselves from reality and granted a creative role to the imagination. And, under the effects of modernity and technology, the language likewise moved away from the body and life. Language has become a raw material to be transformed. The poet has become a manufacturer who transforms words into a product: the poem.

In the conjunction of this original past and this modern technicality is everything that tends to reinforce obviousness and immediacy and to reaffirm the proselytizing and ideological aspect of Arab poetry—that is, its easiness. Arab culture suppressed all questioning; based as it is on the Answer, it instituted a poetry that could say only what is known, a poetry of the explicit. Thus the first difficulty Arab poetry runs up against resides, paradoxically, in the culture of easiness. The discourse of "easy poetry" will be the first obstacle to creation. For that poetry which gives itself over to panegyrics strengthens the repressions and interdictions of the politico-religious institution on which the society is founded. It deepens the gulf that has opened between man and himself, between man and his aspirations. By comparison, all other poetry will always seem arduous—for such poetry will have to begin by putting the language itself to death, as if it were having to struggle against the unknown. As if it had to be an experience of the unlimited and infinite. This poetry has existed at various moments during Islam, and it continues to exist, but it is marginalized and frowned upon. Reading it is not an act of consumption; it is an act of creation. Therefore, after the problem of easiness comes the difficulty engendered by poetic investigation. The light such investigation may cast on the unknown only enlarges the unknown's dimensions, announcing its depth and its extremity as if the light were transforming itself into night. And if this light opens the horizon to the night of the world, the limits it makes poetry cross open poetry to the unlimited. As if the darkness were amplified by the very movement of the light, as if poetry knew only its own limits. The dark world that is illumined is the very thing that leads poetry toward an even darker world.

This unknown is not a meaning that can be grasped definitively. It is mobility, not fixity. Displacing the meanings of words from one horizon to another, writing creates a new space for meaning, a different kind of cognitive pleasure. Disturbing the opposition between the explicit and the implicit, the real and the unknown, it destroys the immutable relations between the signifier and the signified while insisting on other relations having to do with mysteries of existence. The interest of this writing thus focuses on the hidden-implicit and the probable-imaginary, in opposition to the certain-rational. The reader, moving through the realm of the imaginary and the probable, evolves within an atypical writing stripped of references. He no longer enters the poem as he would a garden whose fruits are within easy reach of his hand, but rather as he would an abyss or an epic. Anything he might glean from it will demand a great deal of effort; he will not achieve it with his mind or his heart alone, but with his whole being. This writing takes unmarked paths to go toward that other place that cannot be reached, for it is always in motion and always leads us toward a place still further away. Language, which here abandons the modes and categories of writing, adheres totally to the dynamic of this experience and even to its errancies.

This poetic writing has opened important breaches in the dominant religious and cultural fabric. Expressing the unheard-of and suggesting the unsaid, it has blurred the images both of certitude. Opening doors onto the unsayable, it insists on the absence of any correspondence between things and words, which entails a questioning of the truth of any discourse whatsoever, be it human or divine. It presents a text that is open and unfinished, the opposite of the sealed eternal text of religion. This results in the difficulty I call the "difficulty of interpretation" or the "difficulty of edges." For the language of this writing is that of the boundaries joining the visible to the invisible, the language of the edges which delineate their contours. It is the language of the far away and the peril-

[106]

ous: a language of extremes, a language that flays words and in so doing expresses world.

5.

There exists another form of difficulty, this one linked to the notion of identity, and which is, in Arab society, essentially attached to language and religion. As it is lived, identity engenders a reading based on the nostalgia for an original unity: the unity of the nation, the language, the homeland, and of power. This ideological reading perceives the poetic text as a battleground between ideas and current tendencies: it makes the poetic text a political text. When it is unable to adapt the poetic text to its ends, this reading qualifies it as "difficult" and sometimes goes so far as to deny its status as poetry. Because it unites language with identity and truth with force, this reading ends by confusing knowledge with power. Its underlying concept of identity is univocal in a theological sense and idealistic in a philosophical sense. The essential component of this reading is a separation from the other, a self-sufficiency that gives the illusion of continuity and, in consequence, the illusion of cohesion and singularity with respect to other identities. In Arab society, poetry is the first criterion by which a poet's identity and the extent of his belonging within the society is measured; we can thus understand the challenge faced by a poetry that establishes another concept of identity—one that is pluralist, open, agnostic and secular.

Identity, in this poetry, is not only consciousness; it is also the unconscious. It is not only the licit but also the repressed, the unsaid; not only what has been realized but above all what is possible. It is the continuous and the discontinuous, the implicit and the explicit.

There is a fissure at the very heart of the univocal and phantasmal identity. The unity of the "self" is only apparent, for this self is fundamentally a rift. And the "other" lives deep inside the "self." There is no "self" without the "other." Living identity exists within the fertile, ambiguous relational tension between the self and the other. Without this tension, identity would be that of the thing, and no longer that of Man.

[107]

Identity does not come only from within: it is a living and continuous interaction between interior and exterior. It can thus be said that identity lies not so much in the immutable and the implicit as in what is variable and not yet made explicit. In other words, identity is a meaning that inhabits an image that is always mobile. It evinces itself more in the process of orientation than in any final return. It exists in openness, not inclosure; in interaction, not in withdrawal.

In poetry, the problem of identity is expressed in a privileged way. Identity, in poetic language, is an eternal questioning. In the creative experience, man is himself only insofar as he moves beyond what he is. His identity is a dialectic between what he is and what he is becoming; it is more beyond than behind him, for man is essentially a will to create and to change. To put it another way, identity is less an inheritance than a creation. Unlike other creatures, man creates his identity by creating his life and his thought.

So that within the context of the dominant Arab culture what is called "the difficulty of poetry" does not emerge from the text itself and is not found within it. This "difficulty" stems instead from the level and quality of the culture and is linked to the reader's aptitude for understanding the poem: to his way of reading.

Can't we then say that, within the context of this culture, poetry does not become poetry unless it frees itself from the easiness and obviousness that is demanded of it?

Can't we say: no, there is no difficult poetry?

—Translated from the French by Esther Allen